Little People, BIG DREAMS®
OPRAH WINFREY

Written by
Maria Isabel Sánchez Vegara

Illustrated by
Sera Latterell

Frances Lincoln
Children's Books

Once in Mississippi, USA, lived a bright girl named Oprah who loved books. When her parents separated, she was raised by her grandmother, who taught Oprah to read. By age three, she could even read aloud to their farm animals!

But her grandmother was strict and often punished Oprah harshly. At church, Oprah impressed everyone by reading Bible verses, but what she wished for most was her grandmother's approval. She didn't know it, but one day, real confidence would grow inside.

At six, Oprah was sent to a big city to live with her mother and her younger half-sister, Patricia. But her mum had to work long hours as a maid to support the family, so the two girls were often left in the care of others.

When Oprah was nine, someone who should have cared for her hurt her, and she was too afraid to tell her mum. It happened again as she grew older. Oprah only found comfort in reading.

The stories her teacher, Mrs Duncan, chose just for her helped Oprah feel less alone.

Moving to live with her dad in Nashville gave Oprah a fresh start and helped her focus on school. She joined the speech and drama club, where she loved performing and telling stories. Things were looking up for her!

After winning a public speaking contest, Oprah earned a scholarship to go to university. While studying, she worked at a radio station. Then, she became the first Black woman to read the evening news on Nashville's local television channel.

But Oprah dreamt of being closer to people. She began co-hosting a talk show. There, she listened to stories from the audience. Her friendly and honest style was so popular that she was offered her own show.

One day, Oprah told millions of viewers about the sad things that had happened to her as a child. Speaking up took courage, and it helped others feel less alone. She showed that sharing our feelings is the first step to feeling better.

Soon after, Oprah started her own studio and called it Harpo, which is her name spelt backwards. A big team worked with her on the show. They planned, filmed and put together each episode, making sure it was amazing!

A visit from my teacher (1989)

Touring with Tina Turner (1997)

Who needs pajamas? (1996)

The Oprah Winfrey Show became the most famous talk show in the world. For over twenty-five years, Oprah touched the lives of her guests and the hearts of the audience with some of the most memorable moments in television history.

Men from Alaska (1989)

Mattie: A little boy with a big soul (2001)

Spreading love (2006)

Still, one of Oprah's greatest ideas was to start a book club. It encouraged many grown-ups to read their very first book!

And, inspired by Nelson Mandela – one of her heroes – she built a school in South Africa to help girls become strong leaders.

Whether through a film, a book, a magazine or a documentary, Oprah continued inspiring people to be their best.

She became one of the most successful people in the world and was honoured with many awards for her work.

And little Oprah shows us that even when life is hard, we can plant seeds of courage and kindness that one day grow into something beautiful.

After all, the biggest adventure we can take is to live the life of our dreams.

OPRAH WINFREY

(Born 1954)

1978

2006

Oprah was actually named Orpah at birth, but her name was mispronounced so much that eventually everyone called her Oprah. She was raised by her strict and often harsh grandmother, Hattie Mae. But Hattie Mae taught her how to read, and the comfort Oprah found in books would stay with her forever. Aged six, she moved to live with her mother in Wisconsin. Her mum had to work long hours as a maid to support the family, so Oprah was often left in the care of others. During this time Oprah was harmed by a number of grown-ups. Too afraid to tell anyone, she turned once more to reading. Things began to change when Oprah moved to Nashville to live with her father. She graduated from high school with honours and went on to study at Tennessee State University.

2013   2024

She became a radio presenter and was later the first Black woman to read the news on Nashville television. Oprah found her calling when she became a talk show host – her personal style won the hearts of audiences across America. In 1986, *The Oprah Winfrey Show* was launched. It won awards and ran for twenty-five years, during which time Oprah created her own production company, Harpo. As her success went worldwide, she launched a book club, encouraging others to find beauty and comfort in reading, just as she had. Understanding the importance of education, in 2007 she also built a school for girls in South Africa. In 2013, she received the Presidential Medal of Freedom. Oprah continues to use her success to help people be the best versions of themselves.

Want to find out more about **Oprah Winfrey?**

Have a read of this great book:

Work It, Girl: Oprah Winfrey: Run the Show Like a CEO
by Caroline Moss and Sinem Erkas

Text © 2026 Maria Isabel Sánchez Vegara. Illustrations © 2026 Sera Latterell.
Original idea of the series by Maria Isabel Sánchez Vegara, published by Alba Editorial, S.L.U
"Little People, BIG DREAMS" and "Pequeña & Grande" are trademarks of
Alba Editorial S.L.U. and/or Beautifool Couple S.L.
First Published in the UK in 2026 by Frances Lincoln Children's Books, an imprint of The Quarto Group.
1 Triptych Place, London, SE1 9SH, United Kingdom. T 020 7700 6700 www.Quarto.com
EEA Representation, WTS Tax d.o.o., Žanova ulica 3, 4000 Kranj, Slovenia. www.wts-tax.si
All rights reserved.

No part of this publication may be reproduced, stored in a retrieval system, or transmitted, in any form, or by any means, electrical, mechanical, photocopying, recording or otherwise without the prior written permission of the publisher or a licence permitting restricted copying.

This book is not authorised, licensed or approved by Oprah Winfrey.
Any faults are the publisher's who will be happy to rectify for future printings.
A catalogue record for this book is available from the British Library.
ISBN 978-1-83600-749-4
Set in Futura BT.

Published by Juliet Matthews · Designed by Sasha Moxon, Izzy Bowman and Karissa Santos
Edited by Lucy Menzies and Claire Grace · Editorial management by Izzie Hewitt
Production by Robin Boothroyd
Manufactured in Bosnia and Herzegovina by GPS Group
1 3 5 7 9 8 6 4 2

Photographic acknowledgements (pages 28-29, from left to right): 1. A portrait of Oprah Winfrey upon becoming co-anchor of Eyewitness News on WJZ, with co-host Jerry Turner, Baltimore, Maryland, 26th June, 1978. (Photo by Afro American Newspapers/Gado/Getty Images.) 2. Oprah Winfrey hugs one of the girls who she interviewed for her school for unpriveleged girls on August 10th, 2006, in Johannesburg, South Africa. (Photo by Per-Anders Pettersson/Getty Images.) 3. US President Barack Obama presents the Presidential Medal of Freedom to Oprah Winfrey during a ceremony in the East Room of the White House on November 20th, 2013, in Washington, D.C. AFP PHOTO/Mandel NGAN (MANDEL NGAN/AFP via Getty Images). 4. Oprah Winfrey at the 55th NAACP Image Awards held at The Shrine Auditorium on March 16th, 2024, in Los Angeles, California. (Photo by John Salangsang/Variety via Getty Images.)

Collect the Little People, BIG DREAMS® series:

- FRIDA KAHLO
- COCO CHANEL
- MAYA ANGELOU
- AMELIA EARHART
- AGATHA CHRISTIE
- MARIE CURIE
- ROSA PARKS
- AUDREY HEPBURN
- EMMELINE PANKHURST 
- ELLA FITZGERALD
- ADA LOVELACE
- JANE AUSTEN
- GEORGIA O'KEEFFE
- HARRIET TUBMAN
- ANNE FRANK
- MOTHER TERESA
- JOSEPHINE BAKER
- L. M. MONTGOMERY 
- JANE GOODALL
- SIMONE DE BEAUVOIR
- MUHAMMAD ALI
- STEPHEN HAWKING
- MARIA MONTESSORI
- VIVIENNE WESTWOOD
- MAHATMA GANDHI
- DAVID BOWIE
- WILMA RUDOLPH 
- DOLLY PARTON
- BRUCE LEE
- RUDOLF NUREYEV
- ZAHA HADID
- MARY SHELLEY
- MARTIN LUTHER KING JR.
- DAVID ATTENBOROUGH
- ASTRID LINDGREN
- EVONNE GOOLAGONG 
- BOB DYLAN
- ALAN TURING
- BILLIE JEAN KING
- GRETA THUNBERG
- JESSE OWENS
- JEAN-MICHEL BASQUIAT
- ARETHA FRANKLIN
- CORAZON AQUINO
- PELÉ 
- ERNEST SHACKLETON
- STEVE JOBS
- AYRTON SENNA
- LOUISE BOURGEOIS
- ELTON JOHN
- JOHN LENNON
- PRINCE
- CHARLES DARWIN
- CAPTAIN TOM MOORE 
- HANS CHRISTIAN ANDERSEN
- STEVIE WONDER
- MEGAN RAPINOE
- MARY ANNING
- MALALA YOUSAFZAI
- ANDY WARHOL
- RUPAUL
- MICHELLE OBAMA
- MINDY KALING 
- IRIS APFEL
- ROSALIND FRANKLIN
- RUTH BADER GINSBURG
- MARILYN MONROE
- KAMALA HARRIS
- ALBERT EINSTEIN
- CHARLES DICKENS
- YOKO ONO
- MICHAEL JORDAN